DID YOU BUY the *Lie?*

Time for Truth

DeAnn Clark

To Contact the Author:

DeAnn Clark Ministries
P.O. Box 1623 | Palmetto, FL 34220

www.deannclarkministries.com

I dedicate this book to Bobby Antioch who was told by a Christian counselor that his body condition was a result of not knowing how to talk to God. Upon hearing this, the "momma lion" rose up in me and put me on a plane to Dallas, Texas to meet him and help him break off the lies spoken over his life.

Left undetected, lies change our lives forever. *Did You Buy the Lie?* was thrust into the forefront as something everyone needs to know.

Thank you from the bottom of my heart, Bobby, for waking the "momma lion" in me.

Love you,
Momma D.

Endorsements

What Others Are Saying

DeAnn Clark confronts confusion which leads to wrong conclusions about God and yourself. She exposes twisted truths and the deceitfulness of the enemy and replaces these with the Word of God. *Did You Buy the Lie?* will help you learn to recognize deception and instead walk in the light of God's truth so you can experience all He has for you.

JOAN HUNTER
Author/Speaker
www.joanhunter.org

As a pastor and traveling minister, I often find myself helping people through many issues that are usually centered around a lie they have believed. DeAnn's book, *Did You Buy the Lie?* is a must have for any person in ministry. In a world of lies and false beliefs, it is refreshing to have someone so clearly and poignantly declare truth. Enjoy your journey to truth as you read!

JACOB BISWELL
Author, Pastor, Speaker

DeAnn exposes the lies of the enemy as no match for the Truth of Jesus. She reveals how a halftruth is a whole lie and how darkness is simply the absence of Light. *Did You Buy the Lie?* aids the reader with fresh insight into the devil's tactics and reveals Jesus Christ as the only Way, the only Truth and the only life to live.

PASTOR ROBERT KING
WALES, UK
www.pastorrobertking.com

The only way the enemy can really get to you is through a lie. If he can get you to believe and receive a lie—well it's like bait, and he will "reel you in." DeAnn has a great way to show you how NOT to believe the wrong thing but instead make a decision to receive and walk in the truth that will set you free and release your destiny call. Then your life becomes an exciting adventure.

KATHIE WALTERS
Kathie Walters Ministry
Macon, Georgia

Did You Buy the Lie? gives a good illustration of the tree of knowledge having two sides; one side being truth and the other side lies.

Jesus made a powerful statement: *"The reason I was born and came into the world is to testify to the truth. Everyone on the side of truth listens to me"* (John 18:37).

We are either on the side of truth or we are blind to truth. If we are blind to truth, we can search it out by asking, "What is truth?"

This book will release a divine revelation of THE TRUTH that GOD *"so loved the world that He gave His only begotten son"* (John 3:16a). Love casts out all fear and love also covers a multitude of sins. Love for us caused God to send His son, Jesus, into the world. Jesus is the Messiah who came to deliver us from slavery and to release freedom! This supersedes all lies, half truths, and facts. DeAnn writes, "Freedom is what God planned for us from the very beginning." Thank you, DeAnn, for reminding us of who we are in Christ to empower us into our destiny.

ADAM F. THOMPSON

Co-author of *The Divinity Code to Understanding Your Dreams & Visions*
Author of *The Supernatural Man* and *From Heaven To Earth*
www.voiceoffireministries.org

Everyone of us, no matter how long we have been believers, have taken onboard lies. Some are so subtle that we are likely not even aware that we are carrying them in our hearts. The world around us imparts many of these half-truths in the very culture that has nurtured and surrounds us. DeAnn Clark's new book is timely in identifying and recognizing the limits such lies place upon us in receiving all that God intends for us. I'm convinced that being set free in this area is a critical step to being able to decree and see the kingdom manifest through us to His glory. Well done DeAnn for this easy-to-read and timely word!

ADRIAN BEALE

Co-author of *The Divinity Code to Understanding Your Dreams & Vision*
Author, *The Mystic Awakening*
www.thedivinitycode.org
www.everrestministries.com

Deception is the enemy's favorite weapon. By convincing you to believe lies about yourself, you keep yourself from walking in the fullness of all God has for you. If you believe you are "less than" it is difficult to reach for more. In *Did You Buy the Lie?* DeAnn Clark shares some of Satan's most common untruths (and half truths) and helps you replace these lies with what God says about you. It is time for you to embrace the truth—the whole truth, and nothing but the truth!

WENDY K. WALTERS
Consultant/Speaker/Author

Acknowledgements

Along the pathway in the journey that writing this book has been, there have been certain special people who have marked the way for me. Their love, assistance, and support have made it possible for me to achieve one of my highest goals. I would like to thank each one of them here, for without them this book would simply never be.

Bee Platt

You gave me a prophetic word about
books to come in the future.

Jane Rucker

Whose support and guidance I could not have done
without. Thanks for the laughs and giggles along the way!

Preston Garcia & Tammy Smitherman
Whose artistic creativity, support, encouragement,
and love have been a light in my path. Thank
you for introducing me to Bobby Antioch.

Jacob Biswell
Fellow minister and author, for being an
awesome encourager and friend.

Robert King
For telling me to hurry up and get it done!

Adam Thompson & Adrian Beale
Who have believed in me and encouraged me.

Kathie Walters
For insisting for years I needed to write.

My Family & Friends
Last and by no means least, my family and friends
who have loved and believed in me through it all.

Contents

No one likes to be lied to; do you? It's so easy to label a person as "a liar" and have nothing to do with them. We are wise enough to not trust him once the lies are discovered. If it is a friend who has hurt us, the sting is far greater than the lies of an enemy. Both are painful; neither is generally tolerated for long.

Isn't it interesting how quick we are to draw these lines among ourselves? Yet, when it comes to dealing with lies told us by the <u>devil</u>, these clear lines at once become blurred. Some pretend it's not happening and absorb God's truth and the devil's lies as all one great religious soup. "You just never know what God's going to do," is their answer. God is treated as if He suffers from dementia and the devil is ignored as an out-of-date fairy tale.

Others love God with all their hearts and genuinely want a closer walk with Him. But it gets complicated when they are not clear about what God actually says in the Bible. Somehow the truths they don't quite have a handle on in the Bible get tangled up with what momma or daddy or grandma said. The end result is a twist of half-truths that, in reality, are not truths at all; they are simply lies with a little polish on them. They sound good to their ears. "If it was good enough for Aunt Martha it's good enough for me. But was Aunt Martha really living her life in agreement with the truth of God's Word? Quite possibly not, at least not all the way!

Still others take it the other direction and live in total denial that the Bible is God's Word and His will for us today. They treat it as an ancient literary work and live their lives by the guidance of anything but what the Bible says.

Each of these paths—along with the many variances in between—produces life results far less favorable than anything God has planned for them. We do live in a time when it is so very common to mix truths from the Word with traditions of men. It produces confusion in our hearts and causes many to draw wrong conclusions about God and about themselves.

For the person who believes, for example, that prosperity and wealth are evil and not meant for Christians, it will be impossible for him to ever prosper as a believer. He has opposing beliefs and the stronger one will win out every time.

In order to overcome this lie, this person must find the real truth in God's Word and be willing to do something about his beliefs. *"Faith comes by hearing…the Good News about Christ"* (Romans 10:17). *"And you will know the truth, and the truth will set you free"* (John 8:32). We must learn to tell whether we are believing a lie or the truth of God's Word in every area of our lives.

These words spoken over us and to us, if they are lies, become the path that we take in our lives because we have bought the lie. They ring in our ears and seem forever etched into our hearts. They have come to represent who we think we are. They will remain so until we start to recognize them for the lies they are, break their power, and get set free from their control.

Let me assure you of ten things as we begin our journey into separating God's truth from the devil's lies:

1. God is not mad at you.

2. You do indeed have a purpose for being here.

3. The enemy of your soul has lied to you in more ways than you realize.

4. Your destiny is still there waiting for you.

5. It doesn't matter if you are male or female; the devil has lied to you about who you are; it's his gig.

6. Jesus <u>does</u> have the answer.

7. You need to agree with God and with what He says about you.

8. There is a whole new world waiting for you once the lies are discovered and their power broken.

9. You might have bought a lie, but what you do about that is the important thing.

10. Don't live with a lie: freedom is your gift from Heaven.

For those of you about to begin your journey of discovering what lies you have bought or heard, let me encourage you to take out a note pad of some kind and jot them down as we go. Take the time to carefully consider your own life as you read this book. Ask the Lord to expose the lies you are believing: lies of the enemy. Dig into your Bible and let His Spirit lead you into the truth.

My prayer for you is that you may come into the light of truth in your own daily walk, to recognize the deception that the devil tries to use against you to stop you from being, having, and doing all that God has laid up for you. There is life-changing truth getting ready to come into your heart. I pray you will open the eyes and ears of your heart to hear God's truth as we explore these common life areas where the devil tries so hard to lay traps for us.

Truth vs. *Lies*

I'm going to give you a very strong image that will forever stay in your mind regarding this book and other things in your life. See in your mind that you have a huge apple tree. One side is full of beautiful sweet ripe fruit. If you take a bite of fruit from that side of the tree it always bring refreshing, provides food for your body and soul. That side shades and protects you from all manner of things. That side is called truth. The other side of the tree, while it might look nice, is diseased. Its appearance is disguising a lie. The fruit, while looking good, is filled with half-good and half-bad in each apple. Some apples are filled with things that will poison your body, twist your mind, and change your appearance and personality. Its branches offer you no shelter and no rest. This fruit will cause you to lose your ability in life and send you down the wrong path. That side of the tree is called lies. Which fruit you choose will either send you toward God's destiny for your life or send you down a false path toward destruction: the enemy's destiny. Enemy? Yes, the enemy of your soul, Satan.

Let's take a look at the two sides of the tree a little more in-depth. We will call it the truth side and the lie side. If you would like to take out a notepad and keep score, that's great! If you find yourself anywhere in this, write down the page number and go back to it. After all, in the end, it's all weighed in the balance. This is your life. Which way will the scales tip?

Let the lineup begin on the deception side. On that side we find lies, deception, betrayal.

These are not pleasant words. No one likes to be lied to. No one likes to be deceived. And to betray someone is an ultimate wrong. Little did Mr. Iscariot know that more than 2000 years after his betrayal of Jesus total strangers around the world would still be using his name to express betrayal in a person, calling them a "Judas."

At first glance you would think that the difference between the truth and lies would always be quite obvious. After all, something is either true or it's not, right? Remember both sides of the tree appear equal.

On the truth side of the tree, the Bible teaches us that God is the only true God and that His word is true and will be true forever.

Jesus said that He is truth and the only way to the Father. The Holy Spirit is called the Spirit of truth.

So, if God is all about truth, and that never changes, then where do the lies come from? Satan-Lucifer, the devil, the father of all lies, that's where. Jesus Himself reveals a lot about Satan.

In describing the devil Jesus uses this strong language:

> ... *He was a murderer from the beginning. He has always hated the truth, because there is no truth in him. When he lies, it is consistent with his character; for he is a liar and the father of lies.*

JOHN 8:44

No holding back there! Jesus didn't mince any words when talking about Satan. He wants us to know how the devil operates against us so we can always discern his crafty workings and not fall into his snares.

With equally clear thought Jesus tells us in John 10:10 the plain and obvious difference between Himself and the devil. Jesus calls Satan the thief and that his only purpose is to steal, kill, and destroy. Compare that with His own purpose, *"My purpose is to give them a rich and satisfying life."* The difference is quite clear.

Wait a minute. If it's that simple and clear, why do we constantly seem to be faced with situations that are anything but clear? We are going to take a closer look at this as we continue.

What's the Big Deal?

You may be asking, "So what's the big deal about truth anyway?" Simply put, truth and lies both produce fruit in your life. It should not be a stretch for you to realize that the fruit produced by truth is of a far greater worth than that produced by lies.

When Jesus was speaking to some Jews who believed in Him, He said that if they really were His disciples they would continue following His teachings. And if they did that, He assured them **Freedom** they would not just know the truth, but **is a fruit** it would make them free (John 8:31-32). **of truth.** Freedom is a tremendous fruit that comes from living on the truth side.

Bondage comes in all shapes and sizes and is custom-made to "fit just right." The devil sees to that. Whether the lie is a big one (God doesn't exist or if He does, He doesn't care for me) or whether the lie is a little one (I'll steal that candy; it won't matter), each one is a crafted work of the devil brought to you in a little package (remember the fruit on our tree) that looks good at the time. But when the package is opened and the lie is consumed (when you act upon it), all of a sudden the sweetness turns sour and what follows is bondage, entrapment—zero freedom.

Freedom is what God planned for us from the very beginning. Jesus came to secure our freedom for us. Knowing His Word and walking in that truth is where our victory and freedom lie.

When Jesus prayed for us in John 17:17 He asked the Father to make us holy by His truth, by His word. What does that mean?

In simplest terms it means to consecrate or dedicate someone or something unto God, to transform us into the newness of life in Christ Jesus.

To know your life is set apart unto God is a big deal! It will affect the way you live, the way you think, the way you speak, and the way you act. It will help determine the kind of fruit your life produces! It even helps you become strong when you speak the truth in love!

Of course, you know the devil is always hanging around trying to take all this good away from us. He uses lies and craftiness through other people to deceive us and hold us back from that truth in the Lord.

Are you aware that God has much to say about us in His Word, too? You may not find your specific name in the pages of your Bible, but you will find yourself just the same—as a child of God, as one who loves Him and who is seeking deeper fellowship with Him.

Jeremiah heard the Lord say:

> *"I knew you before I formed you in your mother's womb."*
>
> JEREMIAH 1:5

Wow! He formed you. He put his attention into how you were formed. Do you think if He knew you intimately He would form you into someone who was destined to fail? No! A thousand times no! God Himself set you apart. He has a will and purpose for you, a plan for your very life. Before you ever existed, He wrote things on your heart from His own heart.

Jeremiah also heard God say this:

> *"For I know the plans I have for you. They are plans for good and not for disaster, to give you a future and a hope."*

JEREMIAH 29:11

The Lord has a plan for you (the gift that He put in you) that fulfills you and does not hold you back, does not bind you with lies, does not bring you loss or lack or destruction. His plan for you has always been the same and always will be. It never changes. When He looks at you He sees you complete, fulfilled, and blessed in Jesus. His plan is for you to flow in that gift.

Written on our Hearts

I hear you thinking, "What do you mean God writes things on my heart?" The truth is, there are all kinds of things written on our hearts. What we take as truth becomes written or taken into our hearts. We write on them ourselves. We allow other people to write on them, some good, some bad. Life's experiences write on them. Most importantly, God writes on them!

Our heart is the most vital place within our being. The Bible teaches us that as a man thinks in his heart, so is he (Proverbs 23:7). We are supposed to guard our heart (watch what goes into it) because *"it determines the course of our life."* What we have "written" on our heart has huge bearing on the outcome of our lives—our destiny.

Our heart is truly a wide canvas that can be painted upon in many ways with many different things. And yet underneath it all we have the promise that God has written His divine plan upon our heart—the truth side of the tree. If yielded to, His plan promises ultimate life, ultimate experience with Him, ultimate freedom. That is written in the depths of your heart, too.

God's plan promises ultimate life, experience with Him, and freedom.

How can this be? What does this have to do with me? Mary, the mother of Jesus, must have wondered the same thing in her day. The angel Gabriel visited her one day and told her that the Holy Ghost was going to come upon her and that she was going to give birth to the Son of God.

Now Mary had a choice. She could either pass all that off as a bad pizza moment or receive it as truth and let that truth be written on her heart. The fate of the whole world lay in the balance! What did Mary do? She opened her mouth and said something. She agreed with God's plan: *"Be it unto me according to thy word"* (Luke 1:38, KJV). That settled it; that's what she lived. God's plan was written on her heart in that moment and it came to pass as she walked it out day by day. Thank God for her choices!

Your heart thinks and your heart speaks. That is a powerful way of living! It's the way God Himself is and we are made in His likeness and image. We are just like Him! Look at the way He created things. He saw them in His heart, then He spoke them into being.

Look at your own life for a moment. You can spend time in the Word discovering and exploring what He has said about you. Do you believe that what it says is meant for you today? Are His promises also for you? Or is there something else written on your heart?

To receive His promises fully is to take Him at His word. Celebrate those promises you received through Him! Realize He is the Source of your life. Jesus said, *"Come to me and I will give you rest."* He also said, *"I am come that you might have life and have it more abundantly."* Now your eyes are watching for signs of life, not disasters along the way. The fruit of this transition is experiencing more goodness, joy, and peace. You have just entered the "Three Rs": receiving, resting, and rejoicing! Fruit, fruit, and fruit—good fruit!

It is so important to learn to listen to what comes out of our mouths. It is the quickest way to find out what is written on our hearts. Is it joy? Fear? Pain? Is it excitement for the future? Is it peace? Is it love? Is it contentment? Is it hope? Heart knowledge comes out of our mouths. What is your mouth saying about your heart? Truth or lies? It's important to begin the process of sorting the two within ourselves.

If you are interested in studying the scriptures this chapter is based on, here is a simple reference list. Use this to further your study of truth and lies in the Word of God.

- Psalm 119:160
- John 14:6
- John 14:16-17
- John 17:3
- Jeremiah 10:10
- John 4:23
- Malachi 3:6
- Titus 1:2
- John 10:10
- John 8:31-32
- John 17:17
- 1 Peter 1:22
- Ephesians 4:14-15
- Jeremiah 1:5
- Jeremiah 29:11
- Proverbs 23:7
- Proverbs 4:23
- Luke 1:37-38
- Genesis 1:26

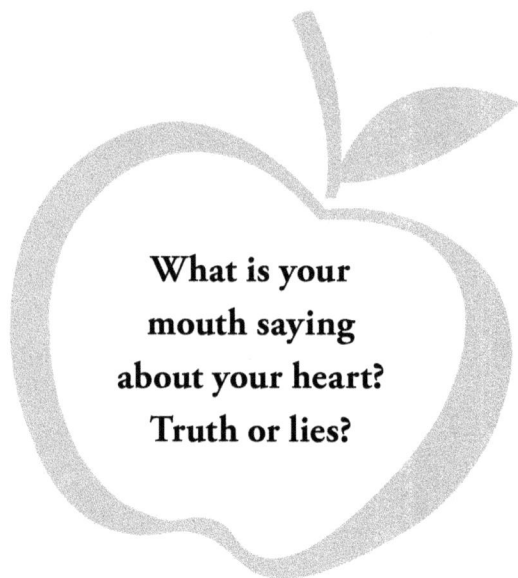

What is your
mouth saying
about your heart?
Truth or lies?

2

Twisted Truth

The Nature of *Lies*

Imagine for a moment that you are a general leading an army in a war. You are bent over your war table with all your chiefs of staff pouring over the maps with you. Strategy is being laid out for ensnaring the enemy, cutting off supply lines, airstrikes timed and ready, ground forces prepared and equipped for battle. Everything is in readiness. Communication lines are in place and operational. There's nothing like a well-oiled military strike force ready to do business!

Now imagine that another high-ranking intelligence officer is bent close to your ear feeding you information from his sources.

This information, as it comes into your ears, causes you to make decisions, to move troops, to set up or call off offensive lines and actions. This "brother-in-arms" so close to you has your heart for the battle. You share the same purpose and objectives. You trust his every comment and suggestion. You move as one.

Now take another look at this war room scene. And notice that this close confidant is wearing a different uniform than the one you are wearing. Take a closer look. The insignias on his shoulders and chest represent a different nation, a different government altogether. Look at the others around you. They are dressed as you and are carrying out your orders. The problem is that your intelligence/information is coming from the very enemy you are trying to defeat! You have uncovered a mole in your ranks—a lie!

Were this to happen in real military life I am sure this spy, this insurgent, would be neutralized immediately, and proper steps would be taken to disrupt everything that he had put into place before being detected. Disaster would be avoided because the truth was found out in time.

Leave the war room, if you will, and re-enter your own life. There is a command center within you—it's your heart. And

There is a command center within you—it's your heart.

there is an offensive action going on in the form of living out your life according to all the goodness that God has planned for you. Decisions are being made moment by moment. At times it gets quite intense there in that command center of yours.

It's great when there is no rush, no pressures coming at you from life. You have time to go pray about anything and everything. Lots of time to sit quietly before the Throne of God and listen to Him tell you what to do in each little situation. No job stresses. No tiredness or illness. No late homework or forgotten tasks. Everything in the world is perfectly on time and dinner came out just right. Is life ever like this for more than just a moment or longer than a dream? No!

The enemy—the devil—takes advantage of this. He counts on us getting too busy or too stressed or rushed or whatever. He counts on us not dialing in closely to the Father and hearing His voice. He waits for us to get out of balance in our emotions and thoughts. And then he strikes. He slides a little thought-note (a lie) across our command desk. It reads contrary to the will and purpose of God for our lives. It twists the truth into something "less than". He poses as an all-knowing, all-seeing, wise benefactor who cares for you so deeply…just trying to save you some heartache, some pain, some time. It nearly always sounds good. Yes, it's a crafty lie meant to deceive.

And if we are not careful and fail to check uniforms, we will find ourselves in the exact same spot as the general we were just imagining. Totally engrossed and committed to the cause, but acting on intelligence fed to us by the enemy. Oh boy, does that describe so many Christians today!

Paul warned us about all of this when he wrote his letter to the church at Ephesus. He spent much of the letter reminding them of who they were in Christ and of God's plan for them. It's an amazing revelation for us today!

The letter finishes up with a detailed training on how to take on the whole armor of God and what to do once it is in place. And he talks to us about the wiles or cunning devices of the devil. He tells us we are not fighting with people. Other people are not our problem. It's not the spouse or child or boss or friend or anyone else that is the enemy. No, we are truly battling with the devil and his forces of darkness and how he is using these people.

God knew we would face an enemy—a defeated enemy, I might add. Jesus completely stripped Satan of power and made a public show of him. The only power Satan now has is power we give him by what comes out of our mouths—which comes from what is written on our hearts and spoken. God gave us His full armor—not just bits and pieces—and told us to put it on! Truth is the first piece of armor Paul mentions here. It is followed by righteousness, peace, faith, salvation, and the Word of God. That's the uniform you should be wearing, and it should be the uniform on anyone in your inner circle!

So are you saying that Satan himself is talking to me and telling me things to do? I just don't get that. Nope! Although I suppose he could do that if he needed to, he doesn't really need to do that. He has others working for him. There are demons that carry out his plans against us. And the most common strategy they use is to turn another person to work against God's plan in us.

Under The Influence of the Enemy

Let me illustrate this for you. Let's say that you have read in the Word of God that He wants you to prosper. You decide that you are going to take God at His Word and believe for prosperity in your finances. So you tithe and sow seeds and believe God for the harvest to return to you. All is well and you are excited to see God move in your life.

Then Aunt Sally and Uncle Bob invite you to dinner on Saturday night. You accept the invitation and arrive at their home that evening. Uncle Bob meets you at the door and welcomes you into the living room. As Aunt Sally finishes up dinner and brings it to the table, you listen as Uncle Bob tells you how horrible things are at the place where he works. "They're laying folks off like we mean nothing. I'll probably be the next one to get a pink slip." You nod your head and smile politely, hoping that you can somehow change the subject while holding on in your heart to the truth that God wants you to prosper.

Uncle Bob gets more comfortable in his chair and starts telling you about how bad the economy is and how much the price of gas and food has gone up. "We don't hardly get any beef anymore, it's so high." The Word of God fights in your heart with the onslaught of negativity flowing in the room.

You seem to be invisible in the room by now as the word war blazes on around you. Uncle Bob continues with the horror story of Cousin Freddy's family's house and how the bank foreclosed and put them all out on the streets and Freddy's boss fired him and the kids are hungry and they don't know what they're going to do. And you can't trust anybody these days.

Your faith is finding it hard to stay lit with the deluge of words straight from the kingdom of darkness. Aunt Sally drives in the final nail when she pops into the doorway to shake her head and say, "Well, you know, money is the root of all evil; besides, you just never know what God's going to do." With that you move on into dinner, leaving your faith plan in the dust of the living room. Mission failed: no prosperity received today.

Were Uncle Bob and Aunt Sally the *enemy?* No, they were not. They were being influenced and used by him, but they were not the real issue. At the root of the whole battle were two things: 1) Your decision to stand on the Word of God and to walk in faith believing for prosperity in your personal finances, and 2) the devil moving against your Godly decision by using other people against you. Notice that it wasn't total strangers he used in this case. It rarely is. He gets far greater impact by using people close to us, people we are open to because we are in relationship with them (our inner circle).

The devil will speak and act through family members (including your spouse), friends, and acquaintances to pull our eyes away from the Word of God and to turn our thoughts away from what God says about us or our situation. He is pretty patient—often more patient than we are. Since his arsenal is limited, he uses the <u>same</u> strategies against us over and over again. Once he discovers what works best against us, he dresses up that same strategy over and over again and runs it by us through different voices and situations. His goal is to wear us down, move us off of our course, get us to take off some of God's armor. Once that happens, he has won the upper hand in that skirmish. We must then go back and retake the ground lost to him.

Still a Liar

Satan is not doing anything new by doing these things. He has done them since Adam and Eve were placed in the Garden. You can read the account in Genesis and see how he came to Eve in the serpent and twisted what God had told them about the Tree of Life. He deceived Eve and she believed him and acted on what he told her.

You know, think about that. The Bible says that Adam was standing right there when it all happened. God had told him to dress and keep the garden. All he had to do was tell the devil to get out of there. That would have been the end of the story. But he didn't do that.

Look at Eve. She could have said, "You know, Mr. Serpent, I'm not sure. Sounds like you might have something there, but I'm a bit confused. Let me talk to my husband first and I'll get back to you." She could have shared with Adam all that had been said, and they could have dealt with it together and helped each other come back to the truth. The truth? Yes! What God told them in the beginning!

But that thing—that thought, that idea, that lie—that the devil presented to Eve must have seemed so true to her and so real that she just didn't even take the time to challenge it. If she wrestled with it at all, the Bible doesn't say so. Even Adam, standing a ways off and observing, was still taken in by some aspect of the lie— that twisted truth—that he was willing to lay it all down for that one bite.

With that one "bite" Satan tried to bite God. The rest is history. The devil was defeated by Jesus and his power brought to zero for the believer. One day soon the devil will be put away permanently. Until then we overcome him by the blood of the Lamb and the word of our testimonies (Revelation 12:11).

Yes, Satan is still the liar. The words Jesus spoke about this are still true. If what is in our mind is not in agreement with what the Word of God says about it, we have been handed a lie—a twisted truth. And it is up to us to recognize it, identify it, break it off, and advance in the truth.

Truth With a Twist

There are various characteristics to the lies that Satan tries to slip through to us as truth. There's nothing new here either, but we must be aware of his strategies. We gain an advantage over him by knowing how he operates (2 Corinthians 2:11). These are a few of the ways the devil tries to cloak a lie in order to pass it off to you as truth to live by.

Many lies fall into the model he used on Eve. "Didn't God say such-and-such?" The devil came to her with smooth reasonings that sounded true to her, but were a twisted version of what God had said. It was a lie in disguise. He does the same thing today with us. Problem: it is a twisted version of what God said. It's not quite accurate. It reaches out to engage you in reasoning, in a debate as to what was really said and meant. Misquoting and reasoning—that's a big strategy designed to sell you the lie.

Any lie from the devil has consequences if you decide to follow it. "You look really fat." In the ears of the one battling with a self-image or self-worth crisis, that lie only urges immediate action with no thought at all of consequences.

Here's a perfect example of how this works. When I was in elementary school all the students were put through a process of being weighed and that weight was recorded along with our grades! They would gather all the children into the school auditorium and line us up for our turn. When your turn came you were marched out to the center of the stage where a nurse weighed you on a scale. She then called out your weight to a teacher across the stage where it was recorded.

All the other children heard everyone's weight. Think about that! I was the smallest girl in my class and my weight was embarrassing to me because my number was smaller than everyone else's. (How I long for that problem again!) My friend had a thyroid condition which caused her to grow much faster than normal. She was always embarrassed because her weight was higher than most of the boys because of that condition. It was a horrifying situation at the time that had lasting consequences into the future.

As an adult still, when she has to be weighed at a doctor's office her heart still pounds and she breaks out in a sweat. She is still experiencing the consequences of what was done. The enemy creeps in through our lack of knowledge and recognition of his strategies. He used that situation to implant things in her mind and heart to cause trauma in her life. He told her a lie and she bought it. "You're fat. You're not normal. You're fatter than anyone else." This destroys self-worth and self-esteem. Has the devil been standing on your shoulder whispering or shouting that lie to you?

> **The enemy creeps in through our lack of knowledge and recognition of his strategies.**

Here again we must stop and ask, "How is it possible that a childhood experience can take on such power in the heart of a person?" Our hearts are powerful instruments operating just like God's does. The Bible warns us to guard our hearts for this very reason—because all the issues of our lives flow through them.

As we continue I encourage you to keep a notebook handy. Each of the following chapters will deal with a specific lie that Satan uses over and over to keep us from God's truth. We are dealing with very common lies in this book, but there are so very many that some will not be specifically mentioned. My prayer is that those other lies that are operating in your life will rise to the surface and become apparent to you as you read. No matter what lie is being used against you, dealing with it is always the same: recognize, identify, break its power, and advance on in the truth. You will see this process clearly and be able to use it in many areas of your life where Satan has tried to hold you back from the destiny God has for you.

Recognize

Identify

Break Its Power

Advance In Truth

3

It *Runs* in My Family

It's *Mine* Now

You have stepped onto the scales and watched the nurse slide the weights across the bar. You squirm uncomfortably inside as she notes your numbers in your chart. Then you take a seat while she straps the blood pressure cuff around your arm. Your doctor's appointment has begun.

Finally, vitals recorded and your chart on the outside of the door, you are seated in a small examination room. Your eyes take in the sterile institutional landscape. A nervousness creeps over you. Even the medical charts and graphs on the walls, meant to educate and enlighten, bring a certain edginess to the moment.

The doctor enters, chart in hand, and sits across from you. And then at some point, the lab results are shared and the diagnosis given. The news was not what you wanted to hear. You have been labeled with a specific disease or condition. Depending on what it is, your prognosis may be less than what you wanted, perhaps even grim. The word *incurable* is a heavy, ugly word.

Your time with the doctor, even if the appointment is long and your doctor is caring and compassionate, does nothing to calm your thoughts. In a blur you walk back out into your life, forever changed.

At this point most people will settle into living according to that diagnosis. Whatever the doctor's words, they now become the final authority over the rest of life. All too often, part of the rationale for this can be: "Well, mom had this and her brother had this and their dad had this, so now it's my turn. It just runs in the family."

Good All the Time

Let's take a moment to reaffirm something here. God is good— all the time. He never changes. He doesn't waffle back and forth bringing good things into your life at one point and then suddenly hitting you with bad things. He doesn't make you sick to teach you something! The Bible clearly states that He is good, period.

Satan, the devil, is bad—all the time. This is vitally important to have written on your heart. God—good; devil—bad. So simple a truth; how easily the heart is distracted from it.

God—Good Devil—Bad So simple a truth.

"Don't you see? My whole family had this _____(fill in the blank)." How easily we buy the lie of disease. How easily we come into agreement with that generational curse and illness.

I knew one family in which every member of the family had cancer. Not just cancer, but a particular type of cancer. In medical terms this is called *predisposition*. It reflects the percentages (the probability) of one's contracting the same illness.

In that particular family it was colon cancer. Every last genetically-linked person had developed that cancer. I mean, you could trace it back. That is actually a generational curse, but it had medical links.

One day one of the family members stood in front of me and said, "Face it, DeAnn. At some point in my life I'll develop cancer too."

Her words pierced the air and I shouted, "Stop! Don't ever say that again. You are accepting that disease right now into your body by your very words. Stop!"

She looked at me like I had grown green horns and had little bells hanging off of them! I, being who I am and knowing how these things work (law of agreement, so to speak) said, "I break off those words and that agreement right now in Jesus' name!" We have been given authority by the power through the blood of Jesus Christ.

Then I looked at her and said, "Don't ever let that come out of your mouth again. Don't ever buy that lie again. Don't agree with it. Don't let it come on you. And if you slip up, repent and get back on track."

What Did You Just Agree With?

I don't know what kind of sickness or disease the enemy has tried to sell you. I don't know if you have a genetic predisposition to something or a fear of something. That fear can also lead to your accepting a condition into your body. Look into your own life just now. Where are you in the realm of disease and this lie?

For example, say someone forgets something because they are super busy or stressed and not paying full attention to what's going on. They get frustrated and bang their head with the palm of their hand, declaring "Alzheimer's!" And follow it up with a laugh.

What did that person just do? They declared something over themselves, didn't they? They are in the process of buying the lie. They are agreeing with the devil that sickness is overtaking them. Now you might think *it was just a joke, so lighten up*. Well, when it comes to confessing something over your life there is no room for jokes. Jokes here can give the devil a toe-hold or permission to move in.

Sometimes I have heard people do this and when I had an opportunity, I said to them, "Stop! Don't ever say that about yourself again." And usually, again, to them I am wearing green horns with little bells on them! If that's the way they want to look at me, that's fine. But they have to hear the word *stop*!

We are also so conditioned by television and advertising everywhere. We constantly hear repetitive messages about certain types of medical conditions that blah, blah, blah.... The next thing you know, you're wondering, *Well, do I have that?* Some poor soul goes, "Well, I saw this commercial about _____ and it absolutely sounds like what I have been going through or am feeling, so I must have that, too." That thought is the seed of a lie. The enemy has planted seeds that can grow up into full-grown lies - to steal, kill, and destroy.

Whoa! What just happened there? That person agreed with the lie of the enemy. Bam! There is celebration in the enemy's camp. Yep, the little devils love it. They are throwing a party because it is moving day. Out comes the caravan filled with more lies boxed up and ready to unpack in that life and in that body.

Is that person you? If so, you my friend, have bought a lie. Identify this in yourself if you have done this. You must repent and break that lie and its influence and impact off of your life and body.

If we are talking about you please pray this with me:

Father, forgive me for buying (believing) this lie about my body and health. Forgive me for speaking death over this body that You gave me. I receive Your forgiveness. Right now, in Jesus' name, I break that lie off of myself. I speak healing and health over my life and body. Thank You for setting me free from that lie.

The Word of God tells us to be watchful so these lies and traps set by the devil for us will not find place in us or take root. We must be aware of their presence in order to refuse to buy them. In 1 Peter 5:8 we are warned: *"Stay alert! Watch out for your great enemy, the devil. He prowls around like a roaring lion, looking for someone to devour."* You must make the decision that you are NOT one of the "someones" that the devil may devour!

Now, let me give you a clue about medical diagnoses. If you receive one, you need to listen and hear what the doctors are telling you about your condition. It's not appropriate to ignore the medical facts, but it also does not mean that you have to receive what they are declaring over your life to be the final word of authority in your life. Ask God for wisdom in your specific situation. Get the mind of the Lord on it.

Case in point. I was diagnosed with something no woman wants to ever hear in her life—breast cancer. I told the doctors, "I hear what you are telling me. I know my destiny (from God) and this is not it. I need some time to get the mind of the Lord on this, so I'll get back to you. Jesus is my Healer, and I will let you know how I want to proceed with this issue."

They stood there saying, "But we need to do something." I told them that I had it on good authority that I had the time I needed to make my decisions. They saw the look in my eyes and heard the authority in my voice.

I personally had choices to make—big decisions. I knew my destiny was in Him. I saw the destiny the enemy had set up before me. I wasn't buying it. I was not buying the lie. I just needed to get alone with God. I had to get the mind of the Lord on this.

I don't mind telling you I was attacked by fear, seeing all kinds of scenarios of what might happen—none of them good. Fear never brings God's thoughts! You have to tell that dumb devil to get out in Jesus' name. And you have to do it with authority; you have to mean it! You have all authority over these things with the name of Jesus. He gave it to you, so use it!

Fear never brings God's thoughts to mind!

Another thing to watch out for is the well-meaning words of your family and friends. When I went home and told my family what the doctors had said, their response was, "Well, look at it this way: you'll be in a better place."

My immediate response was, "I'm not going anywhere!"

Then I heard from them, "Well, those are wonderful words of bravado."

You see, the Word of God teaches that it is what comes out of the mouth that defiles a person (Matthew 15:18). It is what you confess with your mouth that seals your fate.

I already had God's answer on the inside of me. I made my declaration to the doctors that I would live out the number of my days given me by God before I was born and not a second less. The oncologist agreed with me. He took one look into my eyes upon meeting me and said, "You, my dear, are going to be just fine."

I replied, "Yes, I am. In fact, I will slide into Heaven worn out, used up, declaring 'Whoa! What a ride!'"

He laughed with me and replied with a smile, "I have no doubt about that!"

I am telling you this to help you understand that you do not have to agree with what they are declaring over your life. You need to hear what they are saying. Don't be foolish and not listen. But you do not have to receive those words into your life as final authority over your life.

There are decisions you will have to make about your physical well-being, but get the mind of the Lord on those. If you are in a situation where someone else has had to make a decision for you, then go forward from where you are now. God always meets us right where we are today.

Sickness is Not Failure

Here's another thing. It's not a sin to have to make a decision. Personally—now don't ask me why this was so, but it was—I was ashamed that I had cancer. Why? I have no idea, but I was deeply ashamed and embarrassed.

Here I was a woman of God and somehow I had failed. My body had failed me and I had failed God and failed as a person. I prayed for the sick every day. Every Sunday I did not fail to lay hands on people, and those who received were healed. How had I failed? Lord, how did I fail? How could people trust me for a prayer of healing if I was afflicted myself? That battle raged on and on. I had to fight hard to bring those thoughts into captivity and speak words of truth (2 Corinthians 10:5).

These things I do know as truth.

1. No, God was not mad at me.
2. No, God did not put this on me.
3. There is no disease in Heaven.
4. There is no cancer in Heaven.
5. This was not God at work trying to teach me something (another huge lie of the devil). This was the enemy of my soul trying to take me out, trying to stop me in my tracks.

That last lie made me madder than a wet hen, mad as a hornet, left me spitting feathers—to coin a few pet expressions! Here is where I took a look at history.

Kathryn Kuhlman had healings in her ministry every day, yet she had heart disease. Had people looked at her health and not at Jesus, they would never have been healed. You see, she knew the Source of the healing. It was the Healer Himself operating through her.

I decided I needed to get over myself about not being perfect. I knew it was not me doing the work anyway. I knew that all along, but the enemy was trying with his sly little lie to stop me.

During this time as I was walking out my decision-making process, person after person would come to me and whisper in my ear very softly so no one else could hear, "I have cancer." A powerful righteous anger would rise up in me (still does) and I would break off that spirit of cancer and pray for that person to be healed. You have to get mad at what is coming against you, not lie down, roll over, and say, "Oh, okay."

You have to get mad at what is coming against you!

Every time I pray for people like that I feel my heart say, "There! Take that, you stupid devil!" The thief comes to steal, kill, and destroy. Don't take it lightly. Get the mind of the Lord on things, and once you do, do not move off of what He tells you.

There are healings, miracles, and creative miracles out there. Reach for them. If someone reaches for healing and it doesn't come, it's not because they failed or God didn't hear. Please understand this.

Sometimes God says to someone, "Child, I'm going to bring you home." It's His gift of mercy in those cases, His gift of perfect healing. Why one and not the other? I cannot answer that question, and all the healing ministries and theologians I have ever met can't answer it either. We see through a glass darkly.

If you have bought this lie about having to be sick because it's a family thing, please pray this prayer with me:

God, I repent for speaking death over this body You gave me. I break off those word curses that came out of my own mouth in Jesus' name. I ask You to set me free from that declaration that I have been making. I love my body and I speak healing over myself right now in Jesus' name. I break off that generational curse right now at the root. I render it helpless to ever come to pass in my life or in the life of my children in Jesus' name.

Now brush yourself off like you have just been through a dust storm. No, it doesn't do anything in your natural situation at the moment, but it is an act of faith, taking a stand that those things are no longer a part of you.

I will leave you with a few scriptures to help you stand fast against the enemy when he tries to come back with his lies. Won't he be surprised to find his old neighborhood in your body is filled with the Word of God!

- Isaiah 53:4-5
- Deuteronomy 28:15-68
- Malachi 4:2
- Matthew 8:5-26
- Matthew 9:18-30, 32-33
- Matthew 10:1
- Matthew 12:15
- Mark 7:31-35
- Mark 8:22-25
- Mark 9:20-27
- Mark 16:15-18
- Luke 7:11-15
- Acts 10:38
- 1 Peter 2:24
- 3 John 2

4

I *Don't* Deserve It
Why *Bother?*

Have you ever found yourself in a situation in which you really truly want a thing, but you just flat don't believe you deserve it? Something on the inside of you holds you back from even trying for it. It is always a desire deep in your heart—a yearning that pulls you toward a certain thing. Maybe it's a specific career path or finding a certain mate. God puts all kinds of things in our hearts! But the lie says, "You can't have that. You don't deserve that. You're not good enough. You've messed up." And the lie comes with such convincing feelings and "proof" from your track record that you buy it hook, line, and sinker and stop there. You don't even try, and at that point the enemy wins.

It happens to everyone at some point, I think. It is helpful to realize that Satan is not unlimited in what he can do against us. Take a look at 1 Corinthians 10:13.

> *The temptations in your life are no different from what others experience. And God is faithful. He will not allow the temptation to be more than you can stand. When you are tempted, he will show you a way out so that you can endure.*

Temptation comes from the devil, not from God (James 1:13). God cannot be tempted with evil and He does not tempt us with it either.

God has placed limits on Satan. Some folks mistakenly believe (or at least act like they believe) that Satan is equally as powerful for evil as God is for good. They are not equal and opposite forces! God created Satan as Lucifer, an angel in service to God. The creation is never equal to nor greater than its creator.

This is definitely true of Satan. If he is limited to only using what is related to man, then he is limited to the things of this world only. That is good news! Why? Because Jesus told us in John 16:33, *"I have told you all this so that you may have peace in me. Here on earth you will have many trials and sorrows. But take heart, because I have overcome the world."*

Jesus said to take heart (be happy)! Did you hear that? Things will come at you in the world also, but, oh happy day! Jesus has overcome the world for you! You are more than a conqueror! You have overcome the world! Jesus won the battle and gave you the trophy! You come out a more-than-conqueror!

Satan desperately wants us to believe that we are unworthy of anything good. He works hard to make us think we are disqualified from all the good things God has in His plan for us. He wants the Word of God to appear as having no effect in our lives. He tries to make God out to be a liar. But remember, Jesus called Satan the liar and said he was the father of lies. The truth is not in the devil.

That's a great thing to know right there! It follows that if the truth is nowhere to be found in the devil, then everything he tells you is half truth or full-out lie. That makes it simple! Then we just have to learn to recognize when it's his lies and when it's God's truth.

Check Your Heart

In order to effectively address this lie about not deserving good things from God, we have to clear up some misconceptions, some other lies that are being perpetrated by the devil. Satan so enjoys telling us that our past has disqualified us, made us unfit and undeserving of God's good plan for our lives. So, what is the real truth here? How can we have confidence and boldly lay claim to all that God has for us?

Since the time when Jesus walked the earth, there have been traditions of men that declared that this right standing with God comes about because of the good works that we do. That is still believed and widely taught today. And it is a total lie!

In Galatians 2:21 Paul makes an interesting statement. He tells us that he does not frustrate the grace of God by living as though right standing with God comes by works instead of by faith. He explains that by saying, *"...if righteousness **come(s)** by the law, then Christ is dead in vain."* Pretty strong statement!

Did Christ indeed die for nothing? Did His death, burial, resurrection, and ascension have no meaning for us? Don't be crazy! Of course that is not true. That's a lie! So why live your life as though Jesus accomplished nothing for you and you can only receive from God based on your own wonderfulness? Sounds silly when you say it that plainly, doesn't it?

Are you living your life like that? Are you convinced that God has an awesome plan for your very own life and that you can receive all of the good things He has laid up for you? It's time to check your heart as we go forward in this. Remember that Satan is crafty at deceiving us.

So, take a look into your own heart. Are there places where you hold yourself back from good things you truly want? The lie says, "I don't deserve it, so I won't even reach for it." Believing that in any area of your life will instantly and constantly hold you back from all that God has planned for you in this earth.

Believing that lie in any area of your life will instantly and constantly hold you back.

Think about it. What is it that you believe you don't deserve. Is it love? Goodness? Someone that is above your expectations? Advancement? Promotion? Financial security? Anointing? To walk out the dreams of your heart? There are a million and ten (and more) things that Satan will try his best to keep you from having, doing, or being.

God has placed a calling in the hearts of everyone. His expectation is that we find those callings and yield to His Spirit as He guides us into those specially chosen pathways. We are free to choose whether or not to follow this calling, this leading. There is nothing but our own decision-making to determine what we do with that.

So Satan sends the lie right here. "Because you messed up back there you can't do or have that now." When the lie is believed and written on the heart as truth, the life manifests that lie, bringing great pain with it. Disappointment, unfulfilled dreams, chaos, depression, and every other evil thing can settle in over that life. The outcome is heartbreaking.

Jesus became our sin and destroyed the power of sin over us forever. Huge statement, but true! When God looks at you He doesn't see a debris field behind you of all the mistakes you've made or all the sins you've committed. Think about it. If He did that, then Paul could never have stood boldly and proclaimed the gospel of Jesus as he did. In Paul's past lay the grim reminder of all the Christians he had killed or planned on killing. When God stopped him on the road to Damascus, Paul had an official letter in his pocket giving him permission to kill more Christians. When they stoned Stephen, they cast their jackets at this man's feet.

We are talking about Paul, the man God used to write the majority of the New Testament! Did God see Paul (Saul) the murderer, the scourge of the Church? No! In fact, God is the one who changed his name from Saul to Paul. God totally did away with all of Paul's past. And Paul knew it; he accepted it as truth and fact. Listen to him in Philippians 3:13-15:

No, dear brothers and sisters, I have not achieved it, but I focus on this one thing: Forgetting the past and looking forward to what lies ahead, I press on to reach the end of the race and receive the heavenly prize for which God, through Christ Jesus, is calling us. Let all who are spiritually mature agree on these things. If you disagree on some point, I believe God will make it plain to you.

Remember what we learned in Jeremiah 1:5, that God knew you before you were born and set you aside for His purposes? It's true. Paul knew it was true and walked out his life accordingly. God wrote His purpose on your heart, too. He wrote His calling on your heart to be exactly what He designed you to be.

Now that doesn't mean you are called to the mission field, unless you have always had a deep desire to do that. Some people are called to be an excellent mom or dad. Some are called to teach and inspire. Others are called to make or write music, to paint inspired paintings. There are people called by God to have a business anointing, that can direct people in how to build their business or take care of their families. Some He calls into business with a desire to finance those He calls into the mission field!

So, what do you think about your own situation? What is the real reason you believe you don't deserve it? Is it because of things you have done in your past? (Remember Paul's past.) Does it have to do with bad business dealings? (Read about Zaccheus in Luke 19 who offered to make amends for past business sins and went on with Jesus into a new life). Have you been lazy about the things God gave you? Are you or have you been in prison? Did you cheat someone? Not treat your family kindly? What's the devil using on you to tell you that you are disqualified from what God has for you?

> **What is the real reason you believe you don't deserve it?**

Forgiveness Takes Faith

My father was a verbally abusive man. I hardly remember an evening meal without him criticizing, complaining, or being plain out mean to my mother. She would cry at the table almost every night. As a child my stomach was in knots. Supper at our house was not relaxed and fun.

I carried the impact of that abuse into adulthood. It colored how I saw myself and others, and it colored my decision making. Yes, the words and experiences that we are around as kids can definitely have a huge bearing on us later.

In order to become free from all that, I had to release it. I had to forgive my dad, renounce all that, and let it go. That's what it takes to move on when a lie is uncovered. It took a lot of prayer to reach true forgiveness. I will share more about that later. Once I did that (forgiving is done by faith, not by feelings) God did a miracle in my heart. Everything changed! Later in time, after I had forgiven and moved on into God's plan for my life, I did something kind for my father. His response was, "Why are you being so good to me? I don't deserve this." God can and will break you free from any lie you decide to drop.

In Matthew 7:11 a truth is revealed that we must get solidly built into our hearts and minds.

> *"If ye then, being evil, know how to give good gifts unto your children, how much more shall your Father which is in heaven give good things to them that ask him?"*

I doubt there is a father reading this who hasn't at some time or another given great gifts to his kids. Children young and old can come up with long and sometimes pricey lists of good things they want. And it is wired into dad to get it for them. It doesn't have to be material gifts. It can be the gift of undivided attention.

If we are like that with our kids, can you imagine how much more God is like that with His kids—with us? It gives Him great pleasure to give to us and to prosper us. Check out Psalm 35:27. He is our Father!

Even if your child disobeys or makes a mistake, there are consequences sometimes, but the gift is still there and the father's plan to love and give and cherish is not nullified by the child's mistakes. Simply correct, redirect, and move on. God is like that with us, too!

For those of you who do not know or have not had that goodness from your earthly father, I encourage you right now to begin forgiving your dad. It takes courage and faith to do so. And it also takes perseverance. But oh, the release of sweetness in your life when that comes! The freedom that follows the act of forgiving and moving on is life-changing.

The truth is, you <u>do</u> deserve good things, and God wants to give you whatever is good and perfect (James 1:17). Don't buy the lie that says you don't deserve good things. You do because He loves you. Ask God to forgive you of whatever the root to that lie is. Then take a huge step and forgive yourself. Relax and let the good things roll!

**Forgiving is
done by faith
not feelings.**

Chapter Five

Just *My* Cross to Bear

Have you ever heard someone say, "Well, this is just my cross to bear?" It is a saying that is loaded both with pride and martyrdom. Throw in a bit of false humility and attention-seeking, and there you are. You have someone who is going around speaking the lie that they have accepted from the enemy.

Every time they speak that line they are glorifying their disease, their poverty, their lack, and condition of life. Yep, they have bought the whole enchilada! For those of you who are not familiar with that particular phrase, then how about:

the whole bale of wick, ball of wax, hook, line and sinker, or the whole meal deal!

Let me give you a prime example of how the devil steals from you with this little jewel of his. My custom every time I minister is to lay hands on the sick. Why? Because Jesus tells us to do this (Mark 16:15-18). When I am ministering the Holy Spirit shows me if there is someone in particular that He wants to do something for.

One morning while pastoring this particular chapel/church in Florida, I had come into time for ministry. Now in the congregation there was a precious man of God. This man was a retired minister, a precious man of faith. He had come for prayer.

As I approached this man God spoke to me and told me He had healing for him right then. So I spoke to him and told him what the Lord had said. I laid my hand on him and felt healing fire (virtue) go out of my hand and into him. Suddenly while my hand was still there, that fire came right back out of him. So, I kind of shook my head and again laid my hand on him. Again the healing went into him and came back out again.

I looked at him and said, "Honey, it's right here for you; just receive." As I laid my hand on him a third time I said, "Jesus died for this healing." This time as my hand was still on him, he said to me, "You know, my son called me right before church. He said to me, 'Dad, as much as you have done for the Lord, why are there so many things wrong with you.'" Very proudly he continued. "I told my son that this is just my cross to bear."

How I hate this kind of self-righteous lie of the devil! I told the man that Jesus bore that cross for him. Needless to say, as you may have already guessed, the healing came right back out a final time. This man, in his own way, picked up *his* cross and carried those diseases right back out the door with him. He probably added a few balls and chains to his burden as well!

I was horrified and in disbelief at what I had just witnessed. I was very sad when I finally walked to my car that day knowing that God wanted to heal this man, but because he had bought the lie and moved over into pride and martyrdom, he let that gift of healing slip right by him.

Three days later I received word that my sweet fellow minister had died. Yes, the very heart disease that God told me He had wanted to heal in that prayer line at church had taken his life. The healing was there for him. God had desired to extend his life, but he chose to "bear his own cross" and died because of it. I'm sure that once he got to Heaven he was looking back to that very day and saying, "Oh, if I had only seen what I was doing."

The lies of the devil are life-threatening. Very often they are the pivot point between life and death to us. Yet we gloss over them and take them for granted without any thought to finding out if they hold even a grain of truth. Look into your own heart. What thoughts or beliefs are you holding onto like they were a Godly mandate over your life? They can sneak into our hearts without our taking notice of them.

The lies of the devil are life-threatening.

This retired minister, I am sure, believed that he was being humble and sharing in the sufferings of Jesus. Oh dear me, people! That is not what any of this is about. That belief is, instead of being humble, is laced with pride and ignorance.

Yes, the scriptures do talk of sharing the sufferings of Jesus. But think about that for a minute. Please find me the chapter and verse that says that part of what Jesus suffered was being sick and broke and being oppressed. Go ahead. Look. I'll wait...it's just not there!

When we share in the sufferings of Christ it is referring to the Christian being treated by the world in the same fashion as it treated Him. They hated him; they'll hate you when you stand in His name. It has nothing to do with disease, poverty or any of the other things people may think.

I think Satan must love this lie more than most of his others. It makes Jesus look so bad. Unwittingly, he gets this person to speak as though saying, "Look at me. I'm sick just like Jesus was sick! I'm broke just like Jesus was broke. (Jesus was not a poor man!) I'm so wonderful doing His work that I am sharing all his pain and suffering." Oh please spare me! Lies! Lies! All lies! There's not a shred of truth anywhere in any part of that! If you have received this lie, recognize it. We are going to set you straight and get you free.

I had a lady tell me one time that someone had told her that God had made her a beast of burden, and she was so proud of it! What was my answer? Simply, Jesus bore all of our sins, griefs, diseases, and burdens. Once she got through wearing herself out, He would be glad to take them so she could get on with what God actually had for her to do.

Where do we come up with the wrong idea that we must suffer for the Lord, that we must bear and carry and lug anything around for Him? Did Jesus do a complete work in His death, burial, resurrection, and ascension...or didn't He? Yes! He did! He said, "It is finished." It needs to be finished in our hearts and lives as well.

What is the Truth?

In 1855 Joseph M. Scriven wrote a hymn called *What a Friend We Have in Jesus*. Part of the lyrics go:

> What a friend we have in Jesus. All our sins and griefs to bear. What a privilege to carry everything to God in prayer. Oh what peace we often forfeit. Oh what needless pain (suffering, disease, you name it) we bear. All because we do not carry everything to God in prayer.

These words written over 150 years ago are still ringing true today. The song is still sung and played in many churches to this day. Why? Because they are the truth according to the Word of God.

Can you see how the lies are set in place in your heart with the purpose of stealing away your Godly destiny? I have said all of this to tell you that buying the lie that you must bear your own cross will undoubtedly steal your very destiny. It will rob you of your true future, setting you on a path that God did not choose for you. Mr. Sneaky Devil has done it again. He has changed the course of your life.

So what is the truth? I see the lies in these examples, but what is the truth? Great question! Do you recall how we said that Satan always takes the truth and twists it somehow? He is such a loser! That's all this lie is, just like all the others.

In 1 Peter 5:6-7 we find a great insight into both humility and what God expects us to do with cares, or burdens.

> *So humble yourselves under the mighty power of God, and at the right time he will lift you up in honor. Give all your worries and cares to God, for he cares about you.*

Peter is saying to put on humility like clothing. Why? The answer might surprise some: God resists the proud and gives grace to the humble. God resists the proud? Yes! He is not into your prideful bragging about all you do for Him and all the burden that you carry for Him. He's never asked you to carry that! In fact, in these verses we see that the way to be humble is toss all your burdens over onto Him! Doesn't that sound like the exact opposite of the lie that says, "This is just my cross to bear?" Yep! The devil has twisted the truth and you've bought the lie!

In another scripture we are told more about the actual burden we do carry when we are yoked together with Jesus. In Matthew

11:28-30 we find the very truth that Satan has twisted into this lie. (He is so obvious!)

> *Then Jesus said, "Come to me, all of you who are weary and carry heavy burdens, and I will give you rest. Take my yoke upon you. Let me teach you, because I am humble and gentle at heart, and you will find rest for your souls. For my yoke is easy to bear, and the burden I give you is light."*

Here Jesus very clearly tells you that if you are laboring and struggling under a heavy burden, bring it to Him. He takes your burden; you take His rest. He invites you to hook up with Him, to take on His yoke. Why? So you can learn from Him how to live in a way to bring rest to your soul. It bears repeating here that His yoke is easy and His burden is light. His burden is not sickness, disease, poverty, lack and distress. It is love and joy and peace!

Jesus takes your burden. You take His rest.

Even in the Old Testament God has the same thing to say about burdens. In Psalm 55:22 we find this:

> *Give your burdens to the LORD, and he will take care of you. He will not permit the godly to slip and fall.*

What God Declares is True

Folks, God is not a wishy-washy God. He doesn't constantly change His mind about you or anything else. He sets something in place and there it is. Look at the natural world around you to see a prime example of that. Astronomy and all the sciences show that this is true. Read about the creation in Genesis and you see where God speaks something into existence ... and it was so ... and still is. The stars and planets are still right where He put them, doing what He told them to do.

And what He declared true for us is no different. If He spoke into David's heart for David to cast his burden on the Lord and he would be sustained, then He is speaking the very same into your heart today. God is no respecter of persons. In this verse in Psalm 55, the word *suffer* means *allow*. It is not talking about suffering something. God is telling us that when we cast our burdens upon Him, He will not allow us to be moved or taken out by the burden. If you cast that burden on Him He will not allow it to take you out!

Can you see how the Father's heart is so filled with love for you? He wants you to succeed and be happy and fulfilled in your life. He wants only good for you and has planned only good for you. But, oh my, how the devil so cunningly gets in the middle of it to destroy all of that in your life by twisting God's truth into a lie. You buy the lie, believing you are doing the right thing every time. And you get robbed of that incredibly loving plan God has for your life.

Getting you to see the lies you have bought is the first step into leaving the devil's plan behind and moving right over into God's will for your life. You must identify the contracts you have unknowingly accepted that are now set in place and are changing the course of your destiny.

Have you been robbed of health, of prosperity, of loving relationships? Have you been robbed of what God wrote on your heart? Have you lost your way in walking out what God put in your heart? Take a moment, and if you made a list of lies, look at it. If not, right now I pray this prayer over you:

> *"In the name of Jesus, I ask the light of the Holy Spirit to point out those contracts to you. Now Father, in the name of Jesus, I break every lie, every contract off these people. Right now I sever it completely and command it to leave their life, and I send the Holy Spirit to correct their path so they can walk out their destiny in You. Amen."*

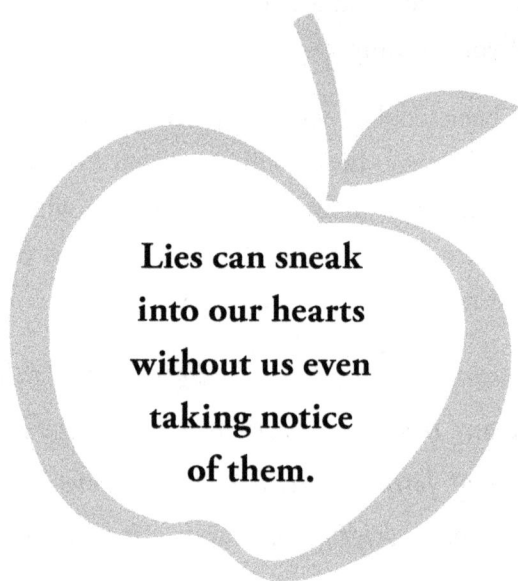

Lies can sneak
into our hearts
without us even
taking notice
of them.

6

I'm *Not* Smart Enough

Have you ever seen a picture – an optical illusion – that can look like two different things? Sure. The one I'm thinking of looks like a vase or a goblet in the center of the picture. Then a longer look makes the image seem to switch from that into the image of two people standing face-to-face. When I look at those sometimes it's a little tricky to get my eyes to refocus from one image to the other. This is all about perception, and perception is very much involved in the lies of the devil.

You'll get no argument from me that education is valuable and important. Always has been, always will be. Take a moment, though, to look with me at a couple of hypothetical but familiar people I think we all "know".

John

Meet John. Nice man. Great job. Loving family. Happy. John goes to work at the corporate office every day and works hard at his desk. The boss depends on him to get the job done. And that's exactly what he does. Were you to take a peek into John's life, you would think, "This guy's got it made! Wow!" John appears to have it all together. And at a level, indeed, he does.

However, upon closer inspection, our friend John has a bit of a dark side. Under all the "great and wonderful," behind all the "got it made" is a quiet gnawing something. On the outside things look good, but on the inside John struggles with fears of inadequacy and of not being smart enough to continue on in this career successfully. Secretly John fears that at any moment the boss will decide someone else in the office can do his work much better. Sometimes nagging thoughts keep him tossing and turning at night. As he lies there trying to sleep he's thinking that he should have worked on that degree harder or gone to that other school or taken that training instead of this one.

Even while John is performing his job well and meeting all his quotas and deadlines, somewhere down inside John is fearful of not being smart enough to keep his job. He is beginning to see himself as not being enough, as not really being up to the task. As he goes along in these feelings, he actually begins to dread going to work in the mornings for fear this is the day the boss will hand him the pink slip.

Of course, following on the heels of thoughts like this come the justifiers, the proofs that make it all look and feel so true:

- With this economy I could be the next one to get the axe.

- Sooner or later they're going to find out I don't know as much as they think I do.

- Robert across the hall is twice as fast as I am at doing these things.

- They'll find a younger guy to replace me.

Our poor brother John is becoming a prophet in his own life. Before long these thoughts become sentences coming out his mouth. At the water cooler he makes sarcastic comments to a buddy about "Yeah, just waitin' for my pink slip! Haha!" At his son's soccer game he laughs with one of the other fathers, "Man, these young guys are starting to take all the good jobs." (Out of the mouth the heart speaks.)

It's not long before John ends up leaving work early one day with a pink slip in his hand, his job falling into the hands of one of those young guys. How did that happen? Did you see that? Poor John bought the lie. The devil that said he wasn't smart enough. John bought it all the way. Bought it to the point of believing it and speaking it out his very own mouth.

Sally

Now let's meet Sally. Oh Sally is a lovely young lady with her whole bright future before her. For all of her growing up years Sally has wanted to be a veterinarian, a doctor of horses in particular. She read so many books about horses and the people who care for them. She rode for years and hung out anywhere she could where horses were around. Her bedroom was decorated with horse figurines and pictures. Her diary was filled with pages covered with her heart's desires.

As strong as Sally's desire was to become a veterinarian, her mother and daddy had some ideas of their own for her. Momma was afraid of horses after having been thrown by one in her own childhood. She worried so at the thought of her little girl working so closely with those big animals. "Why, if they got upset and reared up or kicked, it would kill her!" In her heart of hearts, Momma wanted Sally to become a teacher, not a horse doctor.

Daddy also had his input into the matter of Sally's life choices. He thought it was just weird that his little girl wanted to do something as foolish as becoming a vet. After all, that's man's work and not meant for women. "No girl of mine is gonna go off and do some stupid thing like that!" He'd hurled that and similar comments at his daughter in moments of deep frustration and anger. "Just get over it, Sally." And Sally began to stuff her dreams back inside.

And now, there stands Sally ready to enter college. It's time to move into that dream. But with the new and strange feelings that come with graduating and moving on from what is familiar into the unknown, Sally has strange thoughts and feelings. A hesitation, a swarm of butterflies in the stomach that won't settle down. "Maybe Momma's right. This really would be a dangerous job."

Sally manages to clear the first years of her college career without problems. But once again, the day of decision is upon her. It's time to declare that major. It's time to decide whether or not to go for the veterinarian dream. And sadly, our Sally hears too loudly the voice of her daddy in her head, "That's not woman's work; that's for a man to do, not you." So Sally again stuffs her dream inside.

Back in the beginning when Sally was a little girl the devil laid the groundwork to steal that vision. The lies came through her family:

1. It's too dangerous;

2. You are a girl; and

3. You can't get the education because you're a girl.

The result: the lies changed her destiny.

Both John and Sally suffered from problems in perception. Remember the picture of the vase or the two faces? John's perception choices were to see himself successful in his life's work and happily fulfilled in it, or to see himself being removed from his position by someone younger or smarter. For Sally it was a choice between seeing herself as a fulfilled successful veterinarian or seeing herself as a "less than," a failure.

Take a look at your own life just now. Do you see a little bit of John or Sally in yourself? Is there a similar stumbling block that disqualifies you from living your dream? This is a great time to acknowledge it, if you do, so you can deal with it now! You don't need to go another day with that lie working away on the inside of you!

Settling for Less

How we see ourselves affects us all of our lives. If we are teased by our friends in school about not being as smart as someone else, we forever see ourselves as not measuring up. We don't take into account the motives of that person. For Sally, she grew up with negative words all around her coming from her parents. John's self-doubt held him back. The lie always comes through a voice belonging to someone around us or to ourselves or to something standing on our shoulder screaming in our ear. The devil is a pro at making the lie sound so believable. But it is still a lie!

How we see ourselves affects us all of our lives.

Proverbs 22:6 tells us, *"Direct your children onto the right path, and when they are older, they will not leave it."* A child is born with a natural gift that comes from God. That means that God builds within each of us a certain unique way of going. A good example is our Sally who just knew from the time she was a little girl that she wanted to help horses when she grew up. That is a natural gift that God placed within her before she was born. This scripture is telling us to nurture a child according to the gift from God within him, and the child will live all his life in that gift.

Do you believe God, Who is all love and only love, would place within Sally before she was born a desire and gift for something only to tell her later that she can't do it because she's not smart enough? Would God suddenly one day speak to Sally's heart and say, "Oops! Sally, I made a mistake. Scratch that veterinarian thing. So sorry." No! Of course not! God gave her the gift; He intended her to walk in it.

I think many people live far short of their dreams because they perceive themselves as lacking the intelligence or the courage to tackle whatever learning is required in order to fulfill that dream. They fail to find out what God has to say about them, and settle for something less. But nothing else ever totally satisfies what God placed within the heart before they were born.

Remember we looked at the scripture in Jeremiah 29:11 that told us that God has a good plan for each of our lives. A good plan. Not a disappointing plan. Not a failing plan. Not a pink slip plan. He has a good plan for each of us.

Psalm 37:4 tells us to *"Take delight in the LORD, AND HE WILL GIVE YOU YOUR HEART'S DESIRES."* This verse is telling us to be glad in the Lord and He will give you the things you ask for. That is such a sweet picture of a loving Father doting on His children! There's certainly no fear in that anywhere.

You are very likely aware right now of certain things that you just gravitate toward in your life. Good things. I'm not talking about bad things; those are just sin and fleshly things. I'm talking about that good and strong desire which God placed within your heart, just like He gave to Sally. Take a moment to look at that. What are you doing with it? Are you acting like John, being all fearful that it will go away if you don't know enough or don't perform just right? Have you given up on your dream like Sally, or are you about to?

Stop! Think what the outcome could have been for John if he had decided to use his faith instead of fear and worrying. What a difference! He could have petitioned the Lord and asked for favor in his work and in his career. He could have used his mouth to declare that he was in his perfect work doing what he loved. He could have stood at the water cooler and made comments like, "Hey, I'm believing I'm getting that next promotion coming up!" He could have stayed in thankfulness to God and walked in success and fulfillment.

Sweet little Sally could have thanked her folks for their love and concern, and then taken the whole situation to the Lord. Had she made a stand in faith and decided, "God, I'm trusting You with my life and my career here. I feel like this is something You are leading me to do, so I'm going for it! Please help me get through all the schooling to be what You want me to be," she'd be Dr. Sally today!

John and Sally are hypothetical characters created to make a point. But you are a real person with a real gift burning in your heart, and you have real decisions to make. Have you bought the lie? Have you sided with the enemy against God's plan for your life and decided that you just can't do it? Are you settling for less? Have you already settled?

You must realize that it is never too late to engage—or re-engage—with God's plan for your life. He has made the way for you to live fully and totally satisfied. The key to this, regardless of where you find yourself in relation to it, is to first admit that you have bought the lie.

> **It is never too late to engage— or re-engage— with God's plan for your life**

"Yes, Lord, You have placed something wonderful and great in my heart, and I have let it slip through my fingers. The devil came and told me lies about my gift and what You think of me. And I believed him. I see now that I have been duped. I repent Lord. I renounce the lie of the enemy. I take up again the truth, the vision, the gift You placed within me. I am no longer saying I am not smart enough or I can't do it. I am asking You to open Your door for me now and I believe I receive. Thank you that it is done for me. I will live out what You have placed within me. Thank You, Lord! It is mine now!"

If you just prayed that prayer and meant it, I rejoice with you! You have just taken a huge step in the right direction toward God's plan for your life! Congratulations! Now move forward and embrace what God has put in your heart. Refuse to listen to anyone or anything that tries to trip you up and keep you from the desires of your heart. God is ready to meet you there!

Chapter Seven

It's *Too Late* for Me

I hear a lot of that: I'm too late. Each person who comes to me with this has pretty much the same story to tell me. One will shuffle his feet and look down at the floor. Another will stare into the distance. No matter who it is, they will usually avoid looking into my eyes as they tell me what they are thinking. Then very quietly, almost sheepishly, sometimes painfully, they reveal to me, "I've waited around so long that God can't use me now. It's too late. I'm too old."

This is heartbreaking when you think about it. It's not just a few people scattered here and there who feel like this. There are many. That is so sad to me. How very much God has that good plan for each and every one of us. And how persistently the devil plants his lies in older hearts to stop them in their tracks.

The Bible tells us in Proverbs 29:18 that *"Where there is no vision, the people perish...."* This is yet again proof that people must have vision—guidance, direction, and purpose. In simple terms, we need a God-inspired reason to get up in the morning and face the new day. We become dangerous to the kingdom of darkness when our lives are lived with God-given and -driven purpose.

So, here comes the devil into the scene. He sidles up to you so easy and quiet-like, puts his old cold bony arm around your shoulder, and leans over to whisper in your ear. When you really think about it, you can recognize the moment he slides in there. Before he plants the first thought I think you can actually sense his presence near you. That would be a really great time and place to stop him! But he usually makes it right past your guard. The business of life, the distractions and emotions, fears and chores yell so loud all the time. He comes on the scene virtually undetected.

Have you learned this yet? What does the devil do when he comes slithering up beside us? His nature is to steal, kill, and destroy. He cannot do anything else! What does he do in this case? Of course, he lies! I must say, he is really very good at it. He's certainly had a lot of practice!

If he came screaming at you like a crazy man you'd catch on more quickly that it's him. But no, he's too deceptive for that. He comes at just the right moment when you're at your weakest, when your emotions are wrung out, your body's tired, your thoughts are far from being focused on the Lord Jesus or anything good. And in that moment of vulnerability, bang! He strikes.

"You know, you don't even know how to use the internet like you should. You're too old and tired. Who's going to listen to you anyway? Who do you think you are? You're old and you just have this many years to live (and he supplies you with a shrunken number). It's just too late."

If he gets any response from you at all in your mind—if you play with it for an instant—he is more than happy to continue on with his lie. "You know, back there when you were younger you were supposed to go do that thing for God." And you'll remember exactly what he's talking about!

Then he'll go on once you bring it to mind. "Yes, you missed God. He had something huge for you to do. He was really counting on you, too. Boy, what a dud you are! You sure missed that one! Too late for you. You can't do it now. After all, you're not so young anymore. You've completely missed it and messed up. God'll never get that job done now, and it's because of you. You know, you're really quite useless and dried up. Why don't you just sit down and wait for your turn to catch the bus? After all, you've so totally missed Him there's no hope for you. It's over, loser!" Then he'll "tsk, tsk" in your ear, and pet your head with a little "pity" pat. In the meantime he's rubbing his hands together saying to himself, "Well, I've won this one!"

If he is allowed to carry the lie this far and you are still listening and agreeing and emotionally experiencing his words, you my friend, have bought a very serious lie. To then continue believing that lie and acting as though it is true is to bring untold pain and grief into your heart. And all of it completely based on a lie from the devil himself.

Oh wake up, people! I don't believe there has ever been a time that there has been a greater need for all of us to recognize the difference between the devil's lies and God's truth in our individual lives.

Giving Up On Your Dreams

Here I must confess my own personal experience with this lie. I have taught and ministered the Word of God for quite a few years. And for even longer I have ministered through music. Since I was quite young (not that I'm all that old now, of course!) I had a strong desire to cut an album.

I just felt I was supposed to one day. So one day came. I was actually working with a studio, musicians, and rehearsing, etc.

And suddenly I was in two car accidents in ten days time! (No, I'm not a bad driver!) The first time I was broad-sided. In the second one I was rear-ended and shoved into the car in front of me with enough force to buckle my car.

I had injuries that totally derailed that project. I decided that maybe it was me, just my flesh, and not God who wanted me to cut an album. So I let go of the dream that I would one day cut that album.

I was always "going to cut an album." In fact, I was "going to do" that for so long that the vinyl album became a CD by the time I finally got around to actually doing it! I know; makes me sound like a dinosaur, but it's true. I can laugh about it, but it's true. Just ask my kids and grandkids.

So, I can stand with the best of you and declare, Yep, I said these very words, "I was going to, but I waited too long." I gave up on my dream. I had been robbed, stolen from. Case in point: the CD. At the ripe young age of 60 God spoke to me. As I sat reviewing my notes waiting to minister, the singers were singing. As I heard them sing the words "I see an open door" God spoke to my heart and said, "That's the title of your first CD." I was taken off guard and said, "What CD?" He replied, "Get busy!" Yes, He spoke to me about what I had basically given up on because I had bought the lie that I was too old and it was too late.

At first when it happened, I could hardly believe what I was hearing. I was getting ready to preach in a church in Wales. I had never been in that church before, and I was busy focusing on my message and on what was taking place in the service around me. And in the middle of all that, God was talking to me about CD's?

It startled me, and I have to admit, I was a little irritated at the time. (Yes, I was, and yes, God can handle that with His kids!) So on the inside I just said back to Him, "Talk to me about CDs right before I am about to preach? Are you kidding me, God?"

Not only did He not think much of my remarks, but He also issued His command to me. When I said, "What CD?" He just answered right back, "Get busy!" I was already busy. Didn't He realize that? It was also a shock because the enemy had also sold me the lie that the desire to record was just my flesh.

You see, God had a plan before I was born. Remember Jeremiah 1:5. God had a plan for my life. He set me apart. He wrote on my heart before I was born and He called me according to His purpose.

Not only was God serious about His plan for my life including the CD, but He was willing to continue working with me until I "got it." As my ministry travels took me from Wales into Ireland, He sent across my path this awesome fellow minister from down in Tasmania. It was one of His divine connections for sure. At a meeting there, I was asked to teach; she was asked to sing. So we both decided to go pray. When we met before the service, we had both gotten the same scripture: Jeremiah 1:5. She wanted to change her song and I told her, "No way! God has a plan!" As it turned out I also recorded the song that she wrote, *Before You Were Born I Knew You*, the second song on my CD.

He was willing to continue working with me until I "got it."

Well, God is smart enough to realize how long it's going to take us to get around to actually doing what He called us to do. God has deep grace pockets! So get over yourself! It took me until age 60 to produce that first CD. Now the second one is finished!

Today people are coming to me asking how they can push ahead and get their teeth into the ministry. There is plenty of time in God's plan for me to keep busy until Jesus comes and beyond and then some! The same is just as true for you!

It's Not Too Late

Scripture is filled with examples of men and women whom God used late in life, often with great impact—men and women who refused to use old age as an excuse to ignore what God wanted them to do.

God called on Moses to lead the Israelites into the Promised Land. By the time it was actually time for them to come out of Egypt and into the wilderness on the way to that land, Moses was 80 years old. Think about that. If that were taking place today and God came up to an 80-year-old man and said, "I want you to lead this huge group of people out of bondage into a special place I have given to them," what would that man think? That man might respond like I did at 60: God, are you kidding me? But Moses yielded and obeyed and God greatly honored him. We today are still reading about Moses and his walk with God.

Go back even earlier in time and you find Abram, whose name God Himself later changed to Abraham. God told this man and his wife Sarai—both well up in years—that God had made him the father of many nations. What? Their first response was, "But how can that be? We're too old, God." The Bible tells us that Sarai laughed out loud at the thought of it. (Be careful! Laughing can get you pregnant!)

Cut to the end of their story and Abraham is absolutely the father of many nations. And Sarai his wife did conceive and bear him a son, Isaac, a type and shadow of Jesus Himself. What if Abraham had not believed? What if he had just said, "I'm too old, God," and stopped right there. It is just as costly to God if you stop where you are today and refuse to follow Him in faith and move on into your destiny.

The list is very long in the Bible of people whom God called upon in their later years to follow Him. And in their obedience and yielding to Him, they accomplished His will and purpose through them. So much so that they are remembered eternally in their place in scripture.

There is no reason for you not to join them—and me—in the journey through the rest of your life, doing the will of God, following His guidance every step of the way. Some of you have a big thing to do. Others have smaller-looking things to do. God is not the one putting the measure to things like we do. That's our flesh doing the measuring.

You see, for me it's been making CDs, writing books, and traveling the world ministering the Word of God with signs following. For another it's going down to the school to read to the kids one day a week. Some of you are called to be amazing neighbors and friends and mentors. What is it that Satan has told you you're too old to do? What does he want you to not pick up? What is he afraid of you doing?

Find out what that is, and when you have it square in your heart, tell the devil you have recognized his lie and you're over it! Kick him out and pray this:

Father, thank you for revealing this lie to me. I repent for letting the devil make it sound so true to me. I receive Your forgiveness in this and I let it go. Now, devil, in the name of Jesus, shut your mouth! In the name of Jesus I break off this lie and I declare that I will walk out every last plan that God put in my heart before I was born. God's truth is that He has a wondrous plan for my life and I am right on time! I yield myself, Lord, to Your plan. Show me what You would have me do at this time in my life and I will do it in faith. Thank You, Lord; I am free of this lie!

Congratulations! You have just taken back the rest of your life from the hands of the enemy! God has awesome things in store for you! Relax and rejoice as you move into the rest of your life!

What is Satan
afraid of you
doing?

8

God *Doesn't* Love Me

I've *Blown* It Too Many Times

"We think sometimes that poverty is only being hungry, naked and homeless. The poverty of being unwanted, unloved and uncared for is the greatest poverty. We must start in our own homes to remedy this kind of poverty."

~ MOTHER TERESA

There is an epidemic in the land. I'm not talking about just America, my land, but every land, in every heart. Mankind is in a love crisis. Loneliness, brokenness, heartache, and despair are everywhere. Look into the eyes of so many people and you see the pain staring back at you, standing silent in the shadows just beyond reach. But it's there. Feelings of not being loved, of having no worth or value. The lack of meaningful connections runs rampant in our lands.

Mother Teresa had it right. This love deficit is truly a great poverty ravaging the hearts of so many. It's time to stamp out poverty—this lack of love. How did we get here? How did this come about? If we are going to make a dent in it at all, we must discover the underlying truth, and we must get to the root that feeds the lie.

For such a massive and widespread problem, the answer is not as complicated or painful as you might think. That's good news! Let's take a little time here to look at a few key elements that will unlock the door to freeing the love-starved heart.

It deeply saddens me to hear someone say that they don't think God loves them. "He can't love me; I've done this horrible thing and now I've blown it with God. He won't forgive me and it's over for someone like me." Words like these sink so heavily in the air and drop in pieces to the bottom of a heart. This poor hurting person believes their words hook, line, and sinker. He has given up on God, on himself, on life. He has lost hope.

We were created for love and relationship. For a person to live without loving and being loved is to be isolated more deeply than what he is able to stand. The ultimate isolation is to believe that God has stopped loving you. When you believe that, love is moved out of reach. Thoughts turn you away from love, and then your words start speaking that separation. Before you know it, you have what you've been saying. And you are living life believing you are unloved and unlovable.

Are you relating to this in your own life? Are we hitting a nerve here? Well, first of all, I'm glad that we've found that "nerve" because we want to change it. We want to restore the love to your life that God had in mind when He created you. That is not only possible, it is His plan! Good news, folks!

Next, let me just cut to the chase and tell you the truth right now. Satan is lying to you when he tells you that God doesn't love you because you've done something so horrible He can't get over it. Think about that for a minute. Let that thought sink in. That's a "bad fruit" thought. It's a lie!

Does that really sound like something a loving God would say to someone? Remember He is not just a loving God— He created us for relationship with Him. He created us show us His love.

He created us to show us His love.

The devil delights in getting you to believe that something you have done has taken you out of the reach of God's love and placed you in a dark and lonely place. That dark and lonely place he is trying to get you to accept is really his own "unlove" state! He's trying to con you into giving up the love-filled life God has ordained for you and taking on his loveless existence instead. Wrap your mind around that truth for a minute! Do you see the lie?

I want you to look at a couple of scriptures here. The first one John 3:16 which tells you very plainly that God loves you so much He sent His Son, and if you will believe in Him, you will have everlasting life. As you look at this, ask Him to reveal to you more about His love for you. Listen for His voice and expect Him to answer you.

The Apostle John shares with us:

> *Dear friends, let us continue to love one another, for love comes from God. Anyone who loves is a child of God and knows God. But anyone who does not love does not know God, for God is love.*

> 1 JOHN 4:7-8

How could this man speak so confidently about God? First, he wrote under the inspiration of the Holy Spirit. Second, he had encounters with God! He knew without doubt that God was Who He said He was!

Today we must have that same unshakable confidence in our God. Do we believe all the Bible or just the parts that are easy to understand and receive? What makes it so difficult for us to believe and receive the love God lavishes on us? Lavish is the right word here. How God longs to show us His love.

It's Already Done!

Mankind—all of us—messed up as Adam represented all of us and sinned. Adam's mistake—not tending the garden and kicking the devil out of it when he tempted Eve—wreaked havoc on him and his wife, on his whole family. With the entrance of sin came the first murder when Adam's son killed his brother. Through the ages the whole situation just fell into wreck and ruin, bringing wars and every kind of darkness imaginable. Think about it. God is no stranger to people "making mistakes" and it all started with a lie—**a bad apple!**

Did all that take God by surprise? Not in the least. He knew it would happen way before it ever came about. He made provision for it in advance. He put the solution in place long before Adam ever messed up. In Revelation 13:8 Jesus is referred to as *"the Lamb slain from the foundation of the world."* Yes, God loved you so much that He took care of your sin problem (mess-ups included) before He ever set the foundations of the world. I don't know how far back that was, but it was a L-O-N-G time before you ever needed it! That's the love of God!

The solution was in place long before you ever messed up!

The truth is this: when you let go of the lie that the devil has tried to sell you, when you turn it back in to him for a full refund into your love account with God, God will move heaven and earth to get it to you! It's already done. God is waiting on you to come back to Him and open your heart to receive all the love He has for you. I can tell you for sure, it is more than your heart can handle!

"But," you say, "You just don't know where I've been and what I've done." Stop it! Listen to me! I don't care if you've done drugs big time. I don't care if you made them, sold them, and killed over them. Your drug history is not bigger than the love of God. Your crimes are not bigger than His love. Your hatred for others, your suicide attempts, your abuses dished out or received—not one bit of any of that is bigger than the love of God. There is no comparison at all. The blood of Jesus didn't just cover up your sins; it washed them away.

I hear stories of porn addiction, incest, abuse. I see broken lives; I help loved ones make their journey home to Heaven. The things of this world sometimes are not at all pretty or peaceful. But nothing can separate us from His love. If you feel separated, guess who moved? Guess who bought a lie?

Is that lie that you've blown it too much really working out well for you? No, it's not. It's time to let that go. It's time to know and trust the love of God.

It's time for restoration. Pray with me now please:

Lord, I thank you that nothing can separate me from Your love. I know You have seen all of the things that have kept me out of fellowship with You. I repent of those things and of being out of fellowship, of letting other things be more important than You are in my life. Thank You for Your forgiveness and for washing me clean. I receive Your love for me now. I choose to walk in Your love! Thank You! In the name of Jesus. Amen.

If you prayed this prayer with me, tell the Lord you love Him. My prayer for you is this:

Father, thank You for breaking off the lies that brought separation between this precious soul and You. I thank You that wherever they blew it in life, the Blood of Jesus washes it all away. Freedom in Jesus' name is theirs now. Amen.

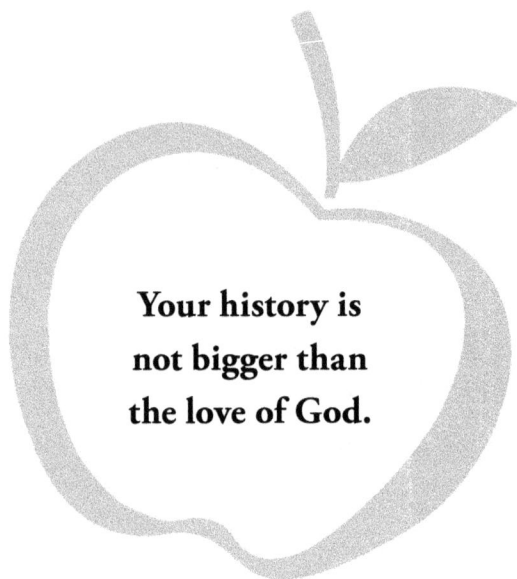

Your history is
not bigger than
the love of God.

Chapter Nine

More *Lies* & The Biggest *Lie* of All

Wow! That's a huge statement: the biggest lie of all. Satan —the father of all lies, the instigator of all deception and confusion, the fallen one—has an arsenal full of lies. The purpose of each, as we have settled/discovered earlier, is to steal, to kill, and to destroy—you and me. He wants to steal God's destiny from you. He wants to take people away from God. He wants to steal God's destiny from you. He wants to keep you out of fellowship with God.

There are so many voices today. We are afraid of some of them. We are angry at some of them. Some make us laugh while others make us cry. Some voices we listen to because we honor them. Others we heed because the voices are wildly popular, and millions of people hang on every word they say. It leads to mass confusion, mass deception. In short, it is a playground upon which the devil is having a hay day, wreaking havoc in so many lives through more of his twisted lies. Huge harvest of bad fruit here.

So many of these voices talk about spiritual things. Building from people's ignorance of God's Word, the devil (always the opportunist) feeds his lies right into their thinking. Remember that bad apples contain half-truths, twisted perceptions, and words.

A perfect example of this is one that I hear frequently when ministering around the world. It may come out in various styles, but the heart of it is the same: "God needed another angel, so He took my baby." No! God does not take babies because He needs angels. He also created people. They do not evolve one into the other one.

Satan uses man's ignorance simply because it is such an easy gaping hole for him to rush through. It's not even a tight fit for him. He doesn't have to wiggle a bit. Any ignorance of God's Word (His will) is an open door for the liar to strut right through and give you a run for your money—your life, your peace, your purpose, your joy, and everything else! Aunt Susie or Grandpa George may have had emotional, sweet-sounding explanations for things they couldn't understand, but they are lies just the same. They simply believed what made them feel more comfortable about that loss.

The truth in this case is so very clear. Read the first few chapters of Genesis to learn how God created everything that was made. You don't find anywhere in that massively creative situation even one time when God said, "Oops! I made too many giraffes. Hey you bears over there, I'm turning you into giraffes now. Sorry."

As absurd as that sounds, that's what a person is unwittingly saying when they say that God needed another angel, so He took their child. We have already established through scripture that Satan is the one who steals, kills, and destroys. Death is not from God. Jesus came to give us abundant LIFE! People, when we die we do not turn into angels. Angels are created beings. If God "needs" more, He can create them the same way He always has.

God's Word teaches us that when we pass from this earth we go on to be before Him. I encourage you to read for yourself 2 Corinthians chapters 4 and 5. Paul is speaking about this very thing. His teaching is straightforward and clear: *"...to be absent from the body is to be present with the Lord"* (5:8). Search your whole Bible as hard as you can, and you will never find any inkling of people becoming angels when they leave the earth.

No my friend, this is a lie. Oh, it's all wrapped up in warm fuzzy feelings, meant to lull its believer into a false state of confidence and comfort. But it's a lie. The devil does not know how to comfort anyone. He steals, kills, and destroys. He'll cushion the lie in soft, feel-better-now ideas, but it is still a lie. Bad fruit!

The devil does not know how to comfort anyone.

Another lie related to spiritual things is the way we get to Heaven. Again we hear many voices. Some say there are many ways to get there. There's a voice out there that says that God wouldn't be a loving God if He only gave us one option. Others say that we attain higher levels of being through our good works or through our sufferings. Please! Seriously? Twisted doesn't even begin to cover this one!

"Oh, but I heard so-and-so say that Jesus isn't the only way. And she's/he's rich and famous. I believe everything she/he says because she'/he's so amazing and loving and kind." You, my friend, are being deceived. You have bought the lie. Bad fruit!

I know this is a topic that draws great criticism and anger. You know the old saying that you don't bring up politics or religion—two taboo topics in polite society. It's been my experience that it's "okay" to talk about God usually. But when the topic of Jesus is brought up, watch out. Things can get tense really quickly.

That used to surprise me when it would happen. Then as I grew in the things of the Lord I began to see it for what it is. Satan doesn't like it when Jesus becomes the topic of conversation in regard to His being the only way. After all, Jesus is the Darling of Heaven. That is the last thing in this world the devil wants you to think. He goes to great lengths to conceal that absolute Truth from you. He sends up smoke and mirrors to get you on a different course.

Religious Lies

Satan has thrown up different religions of the world, each one based on a man or an idea or a philosophy. Each one sounds enticing and those who adhere to them consider themselves elevated above all others, enlightened even. They are blinded to the truth, to be honest.

The list of these is seemingly endless. You know most all of them. When you know Jesus, they are so easy to spot. They are empty of God's love, peace, joy, freedom. Many promise the ability to return again and again, ever rising to higher levels of existence, peace, knowledge, and power. Lies. Lies. All lies.

None of this is new. The disciples and the early Church were confronted with it constantly. To study the cultures and ways of the various cities and lands of early New Testament times is to see a rather familiar sight. It was not uncommon to practically have a temple dedicated to some god on every street corner. There were even places to worship the "unknown gods" in various places.

The earliest converts to the Body of Christ had to learn to discern the Truth from the lies in their day, just as we do today. They had to come out from all that false religion and paganism into the light of the truth of the good news of the Gospel of Jesus. Jesus plus nothing.

The biggest, and certainly the most deadly lie, in the devil's arsenal is now and always has been that we don't need a Savior, that if we do enough good works we'll go to Heaven. The truth is that Adam's sin reached us all, every single one of us. It broke man's communion and fellowship with God. It separated man from God. The truth is that every person on the planet needs a savior. There is only one Savior, Jesus Christ. That little bite off the bad/lie side of the tree separated us all from God. Until we receive the antidote, which is the blood of Jesus Christ, we are not received back into true fellowship. We are considered unclean. We have to be washed with that precious blood of Jesus. He alone is our salvation.

We are not capable of saving ourselves. No other man, creature, idea, or list of rules is capable of saving us. God created us. God knew Lucifer would commit treason and become Satan, the father of lies. God knew that Adam would sin. And God made the way ahead of time for our redemption from all sin through the death, burial, resurrection, and ascension of Jesus Christ, His Son.

We are not capable of saving ourselves.

We are ordained by God to do good works, to walk good paths He has prepared for us. But our good works have nothing to do with getting us saved. They have nothing to do with where we will spend eternity. Good works are just that. Good works.

If the end of your life were to come right now in this moment, are you absolutely certain you would go to Heaven? If Jesus were to come today, do you know you are saved? There is a real Heaven and a real hell, and hell was never intended for any human to experience. It is a place made for the devil and those evil spirits who followed him.

God's will is that we will all be saved. That is His heart for all; that is His heart for you. If you are not sure about your salvation, or if you realize now that you really don't know Him, this is the time for you to settle this once and for all. Some of you knew and loved Him for awhile, but the circumstances of life and the lies of the devil have driven you away from fellowshipping with Him. His lies have heaped guilt and shame and condemnation on your head. You've been told by the devil that the fire's gone out, that it's over. You have been duped, deceived. Let's face it—slimed!

Maybe you've searched for Truth and Life all over the world. Confucius doesn't have it. Buddha doesn't have it. Islam doesn't have it. Scientology misses it. Pick one: witchcraft black or white; Wicca; druidism; Satanism; or any other you might find. They are not the way to God. They are not the path to Life. Jesus is that Way, that Truth, that Life. Jesus…period.

If you are unsure, please pray this with me now:

Father, I am a sinner and I ask You to forgive me of my sins. I thank You for sending Jesus to pay for my salvation. And Jesus I ask You to come into my heart right now and live with me forever. I thank You for my salvation. I thank You for great peace and a great life in You. And I thank You that my name is now written in the Lamb's Book of Life. Thank You Lord. Amen.

If you prayed that prayer, welcome to the family of God! You just destroyed the biggest lie the devil has. He has tried hard to keep you in darkness, but he has failed! Congratulations! Welcome to the good side of the tree!

Final Words

I pray this look at these particular lies of the devil has been helpful. There are so many more of his twisted truths that we could look at, maybe this is just the first volume! In my heart of hearts I felt the Lord wanted me to get this group of lies straightened out for you.

We are living in perilous times. I personally believe, as many others do, that Jesus is returning soon. Now more than ever before God needs His people actively pursuing the things He has told them to do. The devil doesn't want any of us to be free. He doesn't want us active in the Kingdom of God and he certainly doesn't want us walking in the full authority of Jesus Christ!

As you move forward from reading this book, I pray that you will heed the words of Peter in 1 Peter 5:8-9 (KJV) when he tells us:

> *"Be sober, be vigilant; because your adversary the devil, as a roaring lion, walketh about, seeking whom he may devour: whom resist stedfast in the faith, knowing that the same afflictions are accomplished in your brethren that are in the world."*

We have shed much light on the lies the devil uses to stop us. If a lie has stopped a person in his tracks and is keeping him from walking in the Truth of God's Word, then hasn't he basically been deceived? He is not living and walking in life, joy, peace, and victory in that area.

I bless you to continue on in the truths you have discovered in this book. My prayer for you is that you continue to walk in the Light, that you continue to recognize the lies that the devil whispers to you. Remember that he is not going to stop lying to you. He's around til Jesus comes and deals the final blow to him. Don't fall into the trap of thinking that he will just give up and go away.

Always keep before you the instruction that Jesus gave us. He said in John 16:33 that He desires peace for us. *"Here on earth you will have many trials and sorrows. But take heart, because I have overcome the world."* We are empowered to walk a peaceful path throughout our lives because Jesus has overcome the world for us!

Finally, go boldly on your way in obedience to the things God has placed in your heart from the foundation of the world. Pay careful attention to what He has written on your heart with His own hand. Your destiny in Him is great and wonderful and amazing! Always remember to pick truth from the good side of the tree. In short, do not buy the lie!

**Don't you
buy that lie!**

About the Author

DeAnn Clark is an ordained minister, psalmist, author, teacher, and counselor. Moving in the gifts of the Holy Spirit, she is known for the ability to zero in on what the Spirit is saying for a time such as this. It is her desire to see each person have old chains broken that have held them back and be released into their true destiny in God.

Active in the ministry for more than 30 years, she has ministered in a variety of capacities including choir director, music minister, drama and music director, worship leader, and pastor. Through the years she has been involved with Christian Retreat, Norvel Hayes Ministries, Charles and Frances Hunter, Hunter Ministries, Impact Ministries, and Kathie Walters Ministries before launching out into her own international ministry.

Growing up in a small Florida town, the only daughter of a Baptist deacon and a Sunday school teacher, DeAnn began to realize at an early age the call of God upon her life. Recognizing that this call far exceeded the boundaries of her Baptist church, she put herself into a quest for more of God. After receiving the baptism in the Holy Spirit, she began to move more fully into what she knew was written on her heart—into her destiny in the things of God.

Through the years DeAnn has touched the hearts of people from Florida to Siberia and more, continuing to walk through each door that God opens for her. Today God continues to open ministry doors for her from one corner of the world to another. She ministers in churches and other gatherings in the United States, Wales, England, France, and elsewhere. The scope of her travels continues to grow as she follows the Lord's leading.

With compassion and the Word of God, it is DeAnn's mission to bring salvation, freedom, healing, and wholeness to all who seek a deeper walk with Him.

For more information or to invite DeAnn to speak:

DeAnn Clark Ministries
P.O. Box 1623
Palmetto, FL 34220

www.deannclarkministries.com

www.ingramcontent.com/pod-product-compliance
Lightning Source LLC
Chambersburg PA
CBHW071144090426
42736CB00012B/2216